What they're saying about

MISSING ANDY

...

I loved this book, but this is not your usual love story because Andy and Lori weren't your usual couple. I learned this by watching them as my friends in Christ and active participants in our small group. But this is a story in which you can learn a lot about how to deal with life, love, and especially grief.

—*Don Waddell, New Member Minister,*
Southeast Christian Church

Missing Andy is a great example of how faith in Christ heals believers through the grief process. Lori Moore's story is funny, sad, sometimes a bit strange, yet ultimately hopeful. In other words, the Christian life lived out.

—*Bill Womack,*
Louisville, KY

MISSING ANDY

Lori A. Moore

MISSING ANDY
The Journey From Grief To Joy

TATE PUBLISHING & *Enterprises*

Missing Andy
Copyright © 2010 by Lori A. Moore. All rights reserved.

No part of this publication may be reproduced, stored in a retrieval system or transmitted in any way by any means, electronic, mechanical, photocopy, recording or otherwise without the prior permission of the author except as provided by USA copyright law.

Scripture taken from the *Holy Bible, New International Version*®. NIV. Copyright© 1973, 1978, 1984 by International Bible Society. Used by permission of Zondervan. All rights reserved.

The opinions expressed by the author are not necessarily those of Tate Publishing, LLC.

Published by Tate Publishing & Enterprises, LLC
127 E. Trade Center Terrace | Mustang, Oklahoma 73064 USA
1.888.361.9473 | www.tatepublishing.com

Tate Publishing is committed to excellence in the publishing industry. The company reflects the philosophy established by the founders, based on Psalm 68:11,
"The Lord gave the word and great was the company of those who published it."

Book design copyright © 2010 by Tate Publishing, LLC. All rights reserved.
Cover design by Kandi Evans
Interior design by Stephanie Woloszyn
Author photo credit: Powell Creative Photo & Design

Published in the United States of America

ISBN: 978-1-61566-948-6
1. Religion / Christian Life / Death, Grief, Bereavement
2. Religion / Christian Life / Personal Growth
09.12.15

This book is dedicated in loving memory of
ANDREW C. HERMAN

As my husband of twelve years, without his support I wouldn't have had the courage needed to pursue a relationship with Christ and accept his salvation.

Andy entered God's eternal kingdom on September 12, 2008, and when I miss him and talk to him, I remind him to save me a seat!

TABLE OF CONTENTS

Foreword 11
Those Seven Words 15
The Beginning 19
Surgery 23
God's Plan 27
Grief 33
Questions 39
Pain 43
Joy 53
The Bible 65
Comforting Psalms 67
Bibliography 69

FOREWORD

I have often joked that when I married Lori, I realized that I was taking on certain "baggage": three kids (all cats) and an ex-husband. I really like animals, so that part was going to be easy; and as it turned out, liking the ex-husband was pretty easy too.

It seems that everything in my life can be related to three things: the Bible, an *Andy Griffith* re-run, or a *Seinfeld* episode. My relationship with Andy was no different. Our relationship was similar to an episode of Seinfeld titled "The Summer of George," where an unemployed George helped Jerry "date" a girl. Jerry's girlfriend begins to wear him out; she is always on the go, so George suggests that perhaps they team up. The two men had decided that separately neither could maintain a healthy relationship with a woman, but together they could make one good boyfriend. Andy was my George. Lori and he would talk nearly every day about the little things of their day, sparing me (I say this with humor) from being the one to whom she would unload all of the minute details. Then, when it came time to do the things I didn't particularly care to do, he was Andy-on-the-spot. He went shopping with her, to movies, and so on. I used to tease Lori by calling it "Lori's girls' night out" and saying that Andy was her girlfriend. In truth, he made one ugly woman but the best friend that a girl could have.

A few weeks after Andy passed away, Lori asked me if I missed him too. I jokingly replied, "Yes, because he was shouldering half my load!" Then I explained the *Seinfeld* episode to her, and she laughed for the first time since Andy died.

I often comment to Lori that if Andy and I had met under different circumstances, we probably would have been friends, perhaps best friends. He and I got to know each better shortly before he died, sitting with each other in church and going to lunch afterward.

Lori and Andy were better friends than they were each other's spouses, which obviously worked out better for me—and Lori and Andy too. I was blessed to know Andy because I saw in him the love of one Christian for another—he for Lori and she for him. It was and is a great example of what unconditional love can be and has given me the courage to love Lori in that same manner.

It's funny how "baggage" can turn out to be a blessing.

He is missed and will always be missed, and not just because he was shouldering half the load.

Vaya con Dios, Andy

—Michael M. Moore

THOSE SEVEN WORDS

We did everything we could. I'm sorry. With just those seven words, Andy was gone. Five minutes earlier, I had arrived at the intensive care unit waiting room, where Andy's dad and two brothers were waiting. I should have known that things weren't going well when the chaplain came in to pray with us. When the doctor who had responded to the emergency code in ICU walked in, it was just like a movie. Everything in the background faded away. I was sitting next to Andy's dad, Bob. When the doctor walked in, we all looked up as he walked straight over to Bob and said those seven words: *We did everything we could. I'm sorry.* Then everything was silent. He didn't have to say the D word—*dead.* He was talking in past tense. It was obvious that Andy had passed away. While the doctor was speaking, the rest of the room disappeared in a fog. Then Bob started to wail. It wasn't until Bob started wailing that it sunk in with his other two sons just what had happened. They too cried out in pain and started to cry. I was numb. We weren't expecting it. This wasn't supposed to happen. Andy was just forty-nine years old and was fine only an hour before he passed away. The chaplain and I embraced Bob. They say there's nothing worse than a parent losing a child. It's not supposed to happen that way; it's supposed to be the other way around.

Andy hadn't wanted to have the surgery in the first place, much less twice. He had postponed his right hip replacement for more than a year, until the pain was so bad he couldn't take it any longer. He had his left hip replaced in 2001 and was looking forward to a shorter recovery this time due to the new technology for hip-replacement surgery. Andy was scheduled for hip replacement surgery in July, and the plan was for me to take care of him at home. But when his pre-surgery physical detected some problems, his surgery had to be rescheduled—for the same day I was leaving for Kenya for my first mission trip. Andy was beside himself. He didn't want to have the surgery without me there, but he had already planned for his medical leave from his two jobs, and it had taken him so long to get up the courage to have surgery in the first place that he didn't want to postpone it until after I returned. Likewise, I couldn't reschedule or fail to participate in the mission trip. Andy mustered up all of his humility, swallowed all of his pride, and elicited the aid of his father and brothers to care for him while I was away.

At Andy's funeral, Bob told the minister that Andy must have known something bad was going to happen because he said he didn't want to have the surgery. I knew that what worried Andy was how well his dad and brothers would take care of him after he was released from the hospital, not because they wouldn't take good care of him, but because Andy and I had been married for twelve years and been through his left hip replacement, back surgery, and surgery to repair a broken rotator cuff and had the routine down cold. It was so hard to know that I would be several thousand miles away and not be close by if something bad happened and I was needed. Plus, Andy and I hadn't gone a single day without talking for over sixteen years, and I wasn't going to be able to call home for ten days.

THE BEGINNING

Andy and I met in the summer of 1992. When people ask me how we met, I always laugh and say that I stalked him. I had a second job working nights at a local grocery store, and a woman in the department next to mine asked me if I was dating someone. When I said that I wasn't, she said, "There's this guy named Andy that I should set you up with. He's on the fire department with my husband. He works a second job too, up at the convenience store." Then we both got busy with customers, and I never worked another shift the same night that she was working.

But I remembered that his name was Andy and that he worked at the convenience store at night, so I started swinging by the store. The first time I walked in, two guys were behind the counter, so I walked up and asked if one of them was Andy. Their reply was, "No, but we can be if you want us to be." I declined their offer and tried again a few days later when two different guys were behind the counter. Neither of them was Andy. The third time's always the charm, right? It was a Friday night this time, and when I walked in, only one guy was behind the counter. When I saw him, I thought, *Please don't let this be Andy.* He had blond hair—I liked men with dark hair. He wore glasses. The pocket protector and pens in his pocket screamed out "Nerd!" I nervously walked up to him and asked, "Are you Andy?" to which he replied, "Yes, are you the mysterious woman who has been coming up here asking for me?" I admitted that I was the one, told him that I was glad to have met him, and then I left. That's right; I left. I didn't explain to him who I was, why I was looking for him, or anything. As soon as I arrived home I started feeling bad about the whole situation, so I drove right back up to the store to introduce myself and explain why I knew his name and why I had wanted to meet him. We sat down for a while to talk, and we made a date for the next day.

Our first date was horrific. He hadn't dated for a few years, and his last relationship had ended disastrously, so he was pretty negative the whole night. I was sure that I wasn't ever going to like Andy. But he grew on me. That first date had been in July and I had more or less dumped him by September, but we tried it again in December and things started taking hold then. By the following March, he had me hook, line, and sinker.

He was a wonderful man, but for some reason we had a couple of small problems that we just couldn't overcome and we divorced after twelve years of marriage. But once we divorced, it kind of took the pressure off of the problems and we became better friends than we had been while we were married. We talked to each other at least once per day, often more, and we had lunch or dinner or went shopping together at least once a week. He was my best friend. He struggled a little when I remarried, but he adjusted quickly and even started talking to my new husband, Michael, and sitting with us at church.

I was out running errands one summer day in 2008, and when I got home, Michael was lying on the bathroom floor. He had been cleaning the toilet using bleach and was overcome by fumes and had been throwing up for at least an hour before I got home. I tried to get him up but couldn't. There was a fan in the bathroom trying to ventilate the bleach fumes, but Michael was pale and quiet. Michael refused to let me call an ambulance or take him to the Immediate Care Center, so I called Andy instead—without Michael's permission—because Andy was an EMT. Andy agreed to come over right away and check Michael out. Now here's the funny part—Michael was naked! When he started feeling sick and throwing up from the bleach fumes, he got overheated, and he thought that taking his clothes off would cool him down and air him out quicker. I was able to get Michael to crawl out of the bathroom onto the carpet in the hallway, but he was sans clothing. I took a towel and covered him and then met Andy at the door and warned him that Michael wasn't clothed. I'm not sure which one was more embarrassed, but Andy determined that Michael would be fine and just needed to lie still and let the fumes wear off from his lungs. I think this was the turning point in their relationship.

SURGERY

The morning of the surgery, Bob and I stayed with Andy until they took him back for surgery; then I left for the airport. Checking my voicemail from the airport before making the connection that would take me out of the country, I was relieved to hear the good news that Andy's surgery had gone well and that he was doing fine.

When I arrived back in the States, I called home during the layover, waiting for my final flight home to check on Andy. It was only then that I learned that he was not at his apartment as expected but had been released to a nursing home after his two-day stay in the hospital. As it turned out, Andy was a little scared that his dad wouldn't stay with him until I got back and Bob was afraid that taking care of Andy was a bit more than he was up to so they both agreed that Andy should stay at a nursing home for a few days until he was able to be home alone. Unfortunately, Andy had only been in the nursing home for three days when his hip came out of its socket, so he had to be taken back to the hospital by ambulance and have his hip reset into the joint. He stayed overnight at the hospital and then was released back to the nursing home. We spoke by phone at nine the night I returned home, and he told me about all he'd been through during the past ten days. I told him about my adventures in Kenya until we were both tired and fell asleep around 10 p.m.

The next day, Tuesday, I worked until noon and then headed over to the nursing home to see Andy. I had downloaded all of my photos from the mission trip and picked them up from the store that morning, so I took the photos and trinkets I had bought to share with Andy. His face lit up when I walked in his room. I was glad to see him too; I had missed him terribly. We hugged, and we talked, and I showed him all of the things I had brought with me. He liked the two presents I had brought him: an ebony-carved hippo and a green safari hat from The Carnivore restaurant in Nairobi. I got to share all of my photos and stories with Andy at the nursing home where he was recovering, and he told me that he was proud of me. When I fell asleep on his nursing home bed, he woke me up and told me to go home and we'd talk some more on Wednesday. Jet lag had set in, and I wasn't used to the change in time zones, so I called it a day.

At noon the next day, Andy called to tell me that his hip had come out of its socket again and that the ambulance was on its way to pick him up at the nursing home, and he asked me to meet him at the hospital. His brother Rob and I arrived at the emergency room before the ambulance, and we couldn't believe that his hip had once again come out of its socket. Andy was in good spirits when he arrived but was in terrible pain when they transferred him from the ambulance gurney to the emergency room bed. We stayed with him while they performed x-rays and determined that he'd have to be admitted and undergo another hip replacement. Albeit under traumatic circumstances, Andy and I got to spend about nine hours together that day.

On Thursday I visited his hospital room shortly after noon and learned that his hip replacement was scheduled for later that evening. Andy was not in any pain and was waiting patiently to get it all over with. Andy had a couple visitors, so I left, and his dad called me later that night to let me know that the surgery had gone well and Andy was okay. The surgeon had apparently found some bone slivers that were keeping the hip from sitting properly in its socket and had repaired and replaced his hip. Because Andy's hip was so deteriorated and Andy had waited so long to decide to have the surgery, his muscle had weakened considerably—almost to the point of atrophy.

On Friday, still screwed up from jet lag and time zone issues, I was at work by 5:30 a.m. and planned to visit Andy around noon. I missed the first phone call because I didn't have my cell phone on me, but Andy's dad had called me around 11:00 a.m. with news that Andy had been doing well until they got him to try walking and he started to have chest pains. The second call came at eleven thirty, with Bob telling me that Andy had been taken to ICU and that something appeared to be wrong. I was on my way to the hospital when I got that call.

And that's when my world forever changed. After the doctor said those dreaded seven words, he explained to us that Andy had thrown a blood clot, couldn't be revived, and died. It was Friday, September 12, 2008.

GOD'S PLAN

Even before I left the ICU waiting room, I knew that what had just occurred was a God incident. Andy's surgery was rescheduled for exactly the day that I was leaving the country. How strange was that? Although Andy's relationship with his dad and brothers wasn't strained, they weren't really close and didn't see each other often. Andy probably hadn't seen his dad since Christmas, eight months earlier. Because I wasn't going to be there, Andy was able to ask his dad and brothers to care for him. Can you imagine how Bob would have felt if Andy had died and he hadn't seen him in eight months? God made sure that Andy's dad and brothers got to spend quality time with him before he took Andy to heaven. But wait, there's more! God knew that I would be devastated if Andy died while I was on another continent, so he allowed me the opportunity to return and spend time with Andy before he welcomed him into heaven. Second Timothy 4:7 states, "I have fought the good fight, I have finished the race, I have kept the faith." I was so proud of Andy. He had accepted Jesus and was baptized on his birthday in 2002, six years earlier. He had fought the good fight; he had kept the faith, and he had finished the race.

I worked on autopilot for the next five days. I didn't have time to cry; I had things to do. Later that afternoon, I started the process of calling friends and family to tell them the news of Andy's unexpected death. No one could believe it; it wasn't supposed to happen. On Saturday, Andy's family and I met to arrange Andy's funeral. The funeral home director was surprised at our decision, but we decided to hold Andy's memorial service (no viewing), on Monday, September 15, the day that should have been Andy's fiftieth birthday. The family and I decided to try to make it a celebration of stories and memories rather than a sad occasion with crying. After we left the funeral home, I met Andy's brother Rob at Andy's apartment to start going through his things. Having a job to do kept me busy and kept me from having time to be sad. Plus, going through Andy's things gave me comfort because I was with him when he had bought most of them and remembering how and where he got them made me smile and treasure them before boxing them up.

Bob and his wife joined my husband and me for church service Sunday morning. Talk about your God incidents: the sermon that day was on dying, titled *Leaving Boldly*. It was the perfect message that Andy's dad and I needed to hear two days after his death. Psalm 46:1 tells us, "God is our refuge and strength, an ever-present help in trouble." The minister talked about how death is something to be celebrated, not mourned. According to 1 Thessalonians 4:13, we are to remember that we have hope, as it says, "But we do not want you to be uninformed, brothers, about those who are asleep, that you may not grieve as others do who have no hope." Bob and I had hope. We were going to be okay. We also knew what Revelation 21:4 said: "He will wipe every tear from their eyes. There will be no more death or mourning or crying or pain, for the old order of things has passed away."

After church, I headed back over to Andy's apartment while my husband went shopping for a suit to wear to the funeral. I brought over plastic storage tubs and taped names on them for each member of Andy's family. As I went through Andy's things, I thought about which items he would want given to which family member. Andy loved kids' movies and kids' toys, so I also made a box for his little niece, into which I put all of the toys and kid stuff. It made me happy to be doing something good and useful, and again it kept me distracted from being overwhelmed with sadness. While I was there, my husband called to tell me that he was stuck in the department store because there was a windstorm going through town and the store had lost lights and electricity. I headed home, and by the time my husband got home, he said there were a lot of downed power lines and trees across town.

The funeral visitation was scheduled to start at 10:00 a.m. on Monday. At nine thirty the funeral home director called to tell me that the funeral had to be rescheduled for another day because there was no electricity at the funeral home. After some quick negotiations and creativity, I convinced them that we had to go ahead with the funeral service, even without power. I didn't think Andy's family, especially his dad, could handle a delay. They needed to deal with the funeral and get through it while they were geared up to do it. After we arrived, I took down the curtains on the windows in the funeral home's chapel so that there'd be plenty of light, and we opened doors for air. If Andy was watching his funeral from heaven, I'm sure he was pleased to see what a good turnout there was. Andy's current coworkers, past co-workers, family, and friends all came to commiserate the loss of Andy. You couldn't help but laugh when the minister told those gathered at the funeral service that Andy was a stubborn man. When I provided the information to the preacher, who never had the opportunity to meet Andy, I told him both good and bad. I didn't want to do what I think many people make the mistake of doing: making it sound like Andy was perfect. He wasn't. When the preacher said that Andy was stubborn, people laughed and nodded their heads. It was true! There wasn't much crying or weeping at the visitation and service because we all had memories of Andy filled with funny anecdotes.

Andy's ashes were buried next to his mother's plot.

It wasn't until Wednesday that my work was done and I started to feel the effects of the loss of Andy. Whenever the phone rang, I expected it to be Andy calling me. After all, we had talked at least once each day since we divorced two years earlier. He was my best friend. We saw movies together; we ran errands, shopped, and ate meals together. We were very close.

GRIEF

I unexpectedly found grief discussed in Philippians 3:13–14: "Brothers, I do not consider myself yet to have taken hold of it. But one thing I do: Forgetting what is behind and straining toward what is ahead, I press on toward the goal to win the prize for which God has called me Heavenward in Christ Jesus."

I knew that because of Christ, all of our sins are forgiven and we no longer have to live in the bondage of our past, but this scripture helped me realize that grief is also a form of bondage. Grief is probably the heaviest of all our burdens, and God wants us to release it up to him and relieve us of it. While I understand that grief is a natural response to loss, I don't think grief helps us. I think grief is a hurt.

Grief keeps us focused on the past, on the one who's gone, on the pain. Grief keeps us from focusing on God and what lies ahead: eternal salvation and life with Christ in heaven. I still talk to Andy every day. At first, it was because I felt that if I didn't talk to him every day, it meant I had forgotten him and no longer loved him. That was Satan trying to convince me of that, and it was a lie. I was able to let go of the guilt and the grief without letting go of the love for Andy, and now I can talk to him daily with a positive emotional attachment, not a negative one. James 4:7 has the answer: "Submit yourselves, then, to God. Resist the devil, and he will flee from you."

My friend Angie lost her sister a few years before Andy died. She told me, "Grief sucks!" She warned me that people would tell me that time would heal all wounds but that it wasn't true. She told me that in her experience, time just put distance between the event and the wound. Angie felt that the loss of her sister ripped a chunk of her soul away. She described it this way: "This vast, gaping hole seems so large that it's almost visible, almost tangible, almost consuming." She said she remembered sitting in on her first group grief class and listening to people talk about the loved one they lost two years earlier and thinking that those people should just move on and that she wouldn't be still sitting in a grief class two years later. Angie worried that those in the Christian community who hadn't yet lost a loved one just didn't get it. They thought that they were being helpful by telling a mourner that his or her loved one was in heaven, but people who haven't lost a loved one use that saying as a platitude and don't really understand that at times it seems like an empty phrase. It reminds me of a conversation that I had with another friend, Susan. Her mother is as perfect, proper, and demure as they come. A nice woman, Martha has probably never done a bad thing in her life. If Martha decided that she wanted to work with drug abusers, it would be hard for them to find her credible, as she hasn't been through what they've been through. A drug abuser can more easily relate to someone who has previously had a drug abuse problem and then overcome it. That's what Angie meant when she told me about how Christians sometimes try to comfort those in grief but haven't walked in their shoes. She didn't think time heals our wounds, but merely serves as a salve to soften the blow. She shared with me something she once read: "When someone you love becomes a memory, their memory becomes a treasure."

Two thousand eight was an eventful year for me. My oldest cat, Midian, died in April, five months before Andy died. Midian was just shy of sixteen years old when he moved on. Midian had been with me ever since he was weaned from his mother. He was a big black cat, and we'd been through two marriages, five moves, and six jobs together. Although you might think there was a biblical significance to why I named my cat Midian, I'm afraid that there isn't. In fact, I wasn't a Christian when I first got Midian, and his name actually comes from a horror novel by Clive Barker called *Night Breed*. The name Midian refers to the name of the city in the book where the living dead lived. And it wasn't just your run-of-the-mill living dead; it was the weird, outcast, super-strange living dead zombies and creatures. At that time I thought a spooky black cat should have a spooky name. He had battled diabetes for several years and had lost almost half of his body weight. He had developed a liver tumor a few months earlier and was becoming more and more incontinent when we had to make the decision about his quality of life and have him put to sleep. That Saturday morning as I sat with Midian at the veterinarian's office, I sobbed and sobbed. Andy was at work, and my husband was at Bible study. When Andy got home from work, I went over to his house and we tried to comfort each other while we cried uncontrollably. Andy felt almost immediately isolated with the loss of Midian. We had Midian our entire marriage, and he was one of the things that still connected us. Andy was afraid that part of our connection would be lost when Midian left. I once read somewhere that unresolved grief tends to close our hearts down, insulating us from fully experiencing other love relationships.

QUESTIONS

Over the summer, I had intended to participate in a Bible study that was being offered by my church. It was based on the book *Heaven* by Randy Alcorn. I had signed up, paid my registration, read the entire book, and was excited to learn more about what to expect after we leave this earth. But when that first Tuesday morning came around and I was supposed to be there at 6:30 a.m., I ended up hitting the snooze button instead. I figured, *Hey, I read the book; I've got it all figured out.* Boy, was I wrong! The Bible says, "Death is the destiny of every man; the living should take this to heart" (Ecclesiastes 7:2).

Some of my first thoughts after Andy died were about whether he was with his mom, grandmother, aunt, and Midian. My understanding is that our main purpose in heaven is to worship God but that we get to do it with the loved ones who have entered heaven before us. I wondered what Andy looked like without glasses and with the ability to walk straight and without pain. Would I recognize him when I got there? Just what exactly is a glorified body anyway? A movie came out during the summer before Andy died titled *Run, Fat Boy, Run.* Andy used to laugh at this because he referred to himself as "Fat Boy" or "Fat Man" sometimes. When I first started thinking about Andy's new pain-free, glorified body, I thought back to that movie and figured that now that Andy was in heaven, he was probably a perfect weight and size and could run like everybody else. Abraham, Lazarus, and the rich man were all recognizable after death according to the Bible (Luke 16:19–31), and Matthew 17:3–4 tells us that Moses and Elijah were recognizable at the transfiguration. Therefore, I believe that I will know who Andy is among the millions of people I'm going to meet in heaven. I need to keep reminding myself that it's not about my wants and needs or what I want heaven to be like; it's about worshiping God for eternity.

After Andy died, I started to talk to him. Before you start worrying about my mental health, let me assure you that I didn't hear him talk back to me. What I found was that I was asking Andy if he and Midian were now running and playing together in heaven. There hasn't been a single day since he died that I haven't told him that I love him and I miss him. It's funny because the best time to reach Andy seems to be between ten and ten thirty each night. When I lose track of time and don't try to reach him until after 11:00 p.m., I don't feel a connection; I don't feel like he's there. Every once in a while, I will "feel" Andy talking to me in the middle of the afternoon. Sometimes Andy "talks" for a long time, and when he has a lot to say (again, I don't actually hear him speak, but I feel him talking to me) I will cry and cry—a happy cry. I will tell Andy silly things, and I can feel him laugh. Every night I tell him how proud I am of him and how I thank God for the time that we had together. Andy was God's gift to me. I also frequently apologize to Andy for not taking better care of him or appreciating him more, but I can always feel him comforting me when I tell him that, as if he's saying, "It wasn't all your fault; it was both of us. It's okay. I love you." I have no understanding about the rules of heaven, if such things exist. For example, I don't know if our departed loved ones are allowed to look down and watch us, sort of like reality earth television.

Andy and I once stayed the weekend at a hotel in Savannah, Georgia, that was along the river. There was this small light on the wall next to the bed that sometimes flashed red, but we had no idea why it was doing that. When I called down to the front desk to inquire about it, they explained that the light was a signal for when barges were going by on the river outside the window. The hotel had installed the signal lights in all rooms facing the river because guests liked to watch the barges. Since Andy's death, I've wondered if he has a light in his room in heaven that flashes when I'm thinking about him or talking to him. I guess it would be like heaven's version of an answering machine. I wonder if he can hear the words I'm saying or whether he just knows that I'm talking to him. In my relationship with God, I know when God is talking to me in two ways: on my heart and through my tears. I'm not trying to ascribe supernatural powers to Andy, but when I talk to Andy, I get tears. Not run-of-the-mill tears like when I cry about other things, but special Andy-is-talking-to-me tears.

PAIN

While it didn't surprise me to grieve over Andy, there were some aspects that affected me that I could not have foreseen. When you lose a family member, you are the grieving daughter or niece or sister. But what are you when you're the ex-wife? Nobody got it. Some responded with, "Oh, your ex-husband died? But you were divorced and are remarried now, right? Why would losing your ex-husband make you sad?" Okay, nobody actually said that to me, but that's what it felt like. I wasn't the grieving widow, and I wasn't family. I felt like I lacked the legitimacy to grieve my loss. Although I had the opportunity to see Andy before he died and we didn't leave any unfinished business, I somehow felt as though there was this perception by others that I shouldn't really feel a void. Andy's and my relationship was uncomplicated and genuine, but his loss created a level of complication due to the lack of a socially defined relationship. My grief was complicated by my concerns about the perception of others about our relationship. I didn't doubt my connection to Andy, but I felt as though others did.

In the movie *My Cousin Vinny*, there's a scene involving Marisa Tomei and Joe Pesci where the main character, Vinny (played by Joe Pesci), is under a lot of stress. He's an inexperienced trial lawyer, his cousin has been charged with murder, and it's all on his shoulders to save the day. He and his girlfriend are at a cabin in the woods when Marisa Tomei decides to tell Joe Pesci that her biological clock is ticking and that she needs him to win this trial so that they can get married because he said he wouldn't marry her until he'd won a case. Vinny looks at her and says something to the effect that he's already under enough stress due to the trial and his lack of experience. Now that she's bringing up her ticking biological clock, he asks her if there's any other *stuff* she could possibly pile up on him at that time. After Andy died, the same thing happened to me. Apparently, losing my best friend wasn't enough; more was going to be piled up on me.

When Andy and I were married, we had wills drawn up whereby we each handled the other's estate. After the divorce we talked about it numerous times, and Andy wanted me to continue to serve as the executrix of his will because I was the person he trusted the most and knew the best. But when I went to a lawyer to start the probate process in order to settle Andy's estate, the attorney told me that, according to the law, I couldn't do it. The will had been made prior to the divorce, and I was no longer his wife; therefore, it was as if I were dead in the eyes of the law and I couldn't serve to handle his estate. Neither Andy nor I knew there were legal formalities like that. The lawyer said that Andy should have changed his will after we divorced. We had no idea of the legal ramifications of our divorce on other documents. Andy just knew that he didn't want anything to change just because we had divorced. I was devastated. I was the one who was with Andy when he admired his collectibles, and I was with him when the vacation photos were taken, and I was with him when he bought everything that he had. I didn't want his stuff; I just couldn't handle the fact that other people were going to be pawing through Andy's personal things without knowing any of the history or stories behind how they were acquired. Andy's brothers made a couple of comments, including, "Where did Andy get all this junk? Why was he keeping so much old stuff?" They even discussed having a yard sale to dispose of Andy's items that they didn't like. That thought revolted me! I could not imagine seeing strangers lifting up items that Andy held sentimental attachment to and asking, "Would you take a quarter for this?" I know that material things aren't important, but it's tough seeing other people make value judgments about items that someone else held dear. Suddenly, not only had I just lost Andy, but it was also as if I no longer existed according to the law. And then there were the questions about Andy's estate and insurance policies. Andy had named me as a beneficiary on some things both while we were still married and after we had divorced. There was no question about that. Nevertheless, I was asked by his family to consider giving all or at least half of the money to them. Each of Andy's brothers had a daughter, and they asked me to give the money to the kids. As politely and respectfully as I could, I explained to his family that Andy was a grown man who had made his own informed decisions about where he wanted the money to go and I wasn't going to second-guess him or change his plans. It wasn't supposed to be about what they wanted or whom they felt should have the money. It was about what Andy wanted. It was hard enough dealing with not having Andy to talk to every day, but now I had to deal with his "real family" thinking that I, the ex-wife, should give them Andy's money. I have always felt lucky to have had Andy as a husband and lucky to have his dad and brothers as family. I especially loved his youngest brother, whom I respected and had always found to be smart, funny, and dependable. I never thought that our divorce had separated me from his family or that they had any bad feelings toward me. Now, though, it seemed as if things had turned into them versus me, and it really hurt.

Although it may seem strange of me to share the story about my experience dealing with Andy's estate and how uncomfortable and upset I felt about not being part of Andy's family anymore, it was important for me to include that in this book. I want others to learn from what I went through. It's one of my reasons for writing this book—to help others who are in the same or similar situations. Death is hard, but the people who are still living will sometimes make it even harder for you. Somebody once told me that there wouldn't be silly laws against things if silly people hadn't actually tried to do the thing that caused the law to be created. For example, there wouldn't be a law against marrying your sibling unless somebody had actually tried to marry his or her own sibling. The same thing goes for a saying I had often heard, but never experienced: "It's all about the money when somebody dies." I didn't believe it was true until Andy died and I saw it firsthand. It's going to happen. Count on it. Bank on it. Be prepared for it. Stay strong and do what the person you lost wanted you to do; don't give in to the pressure of remaining family or friends who will try to play on your emotions to convince you to do something that they want for themselves.

My brother was one of the biggest helps in getting me through my anxiety over how Andy's family treated me after he died. He did it with one simple question. "Lori," he asked me, "do you expect to have an ongoing relationship with Andy's family now that he's gone?" The answer was, unfortunately, no. After the divorce, the family hadn't stayed in touch with me. Heck, the family hadn't even stayed in touch with Andy all that much! Realizing that Andy's family wasn't going to remain in a long-term relationship with me helped me to understand and deal with the situation much more effectively.

The holidays were extremely hard. Just a month after Andy's death was Halloween. Halloween was one of those holidays that we both got such a kick out of decorating and collecting spooky stuff. Every time I looked at a newspaper ad featuring Halloween decorations, I cried. When I went shopping, I refused to explore the Halloween aisles at any of the other stores.

Christmas was even harder. Andy was a collector, aka a packrat. Making a list of items he didn't collect would be a much shorter list than that of what he did collect. He had boxes of fire truck collectibles, silver dollars, fire department patches, fire-related pins, beanie babies, Christmas ornaments, M&M dispensers and tins, and much more. At Christmas, he especially coveted anything with the Grinch, the Abominable Snowman, or Charlie Brown. I couldn't walk five yards in a discount store or watch thirty minutes of television that didn't include ads for those items. Even after we divorced, Andy and I got together on Christmas morning to exchange gifts in our pajamas. This was my first Christmas without Andy in sixteen years.

My birthday was next. Birthdays have always been special to me because they represent that one day of celebration that is uniquely mine. Andy always got me flowers for my birthday. It was my first birthday without him in sixteen years. I had a vacation coming up—a cruise to Alaska with my husband, Michael. Michael had never cruised and was a little concerned about whether or not he would get seasick. Andy and I had taken six or eight cruises together, and it was our favorite type of vacation. Andy had always wanted to see Alaska and was considering coming with us when we took our trip. I warned Michael that I'd probably cry when we got on the ship because it would be my first cruise without Andy.

That's something I find interesting about grief. I've started keeping track of time in terms not of the date or year, but whether it was before Andy died or after. Every occasion ends up being a first without Andy: my first vacation without Andy, my first time going to church without Andy being there, my first time catching a cold without Andy bringing me medicine or taking my temperature. Am I going to be counting things like that the rest of my life? Christians aren't afraid of death because we know we will see all of our loved ones who have died in Christ once again. But we grieve the loss of those who left before us.

Another unique aspect of my grief over Andy's death is my relationship with my husband. I didn't know he had it in him. Michael has been saint-like in handling my loss of Andy. Can you imagine him having to hear me say, "This is the place Andy and I went that time," or, "Andy and I used to shop here" and "When Andy and I planned things like this, we used to do it this way"? Talking about Andy and sharing memories of him helps me through my grief, but it also makes me feel guilty for talking so frequently about adventures with my former husband to my current husband. My friend Rick didn't know either Andy or Michael very well, but he came to the funeral. A few weeks later, Rick and I were having lunch, and he said, "I have a lot of respect for Michael. I don't know he made it through that funeral." I hadn't even thought about the possible discomfort Michael might have felt. All of the mourners at the funeral were either Andy's family or friends we had together when we were married. Michael didn't know anyone there. He was in the very difficult position of being introduced to Andy's family during his funeral, which was the first time I had seen Andy's family since our divorce. I don't know if there was any ill will there or whether anyone looked at Michael in a funny way because I was oblivious to it. In retrospect, I can see just how awkward it must have been for him and how unusual my continued relationship with Andy must have seemed. Both of our lives were forever changed with those seven little words.

JOY

Then I recalled another time when my life was forever changed. It was in October of 2000 when I accepted Jesus as my Lord and Savior and was baptized. I knew that I couldn't get through my grief alone, even with the help of my wonderful, loving husband, so I turned to God for help more than ever before. God provided me comfort, peace, and the strength to handle going on day after day. St. Augustine said, "When God is our strength, it is strength indeed; when our strength is our own, it is only weakness." My grief isn't bigger than my God. God is bigger than any problem that I could ever face, bigger than my pain and sadness. A phrase that came to mind to comfort me was the phrase "This too shall pass," but I'm really not sure about the origin of that phrase, as I've read different stories about how it came into use. According to author Beth Moore (no relation!), "We are never stronger than the moment we admit we are weak."

Psychiatrist Elisabeth Kübler-Ross introduced

the five stages of grief in 1969. You've probably heard of them: denial, anger, bargaining, depression, and acceptance. I didn't go through all of those stages, and I certainly didn't go through them in that order. I don't think it's a requirement that we go through all the stages because there's no required or typical response. We all grieve differently. My first stage was acceptance. Knowing that the occurrences leading up to Andy's death were God incidents, I accepted that Andy was in a much better place. Does that sound impossible to you? Oswald Chambers says, "The impossible is exactly what God does." Andy was fine; me, not so much. I've heard that a lot of people ask God why he took away the person that has died, but I didn't ask why. I like the expression, "Don't put a question mark where God has put a period." God cares about grammar? Yes, in a way he does. I knew that earth was not the final goal and that heaven was the ultimate prize. I was even grateful that Andy had died in the manner he had, without prolonged suffering. You know how men are about their pride. A prolonged illness that left him dependent upon others to care for him or diminished him physically would have really hurt him emotionally.

Denial surprised me a little bit. After the doctor told us that Andy had passed away, the chaplain allowed us to go back to see Andy in his ICU room. Andy looked good. He looked at peace. I remember taking his hand in mine and talking to him and then leaning over and kissing him on the cheek. He was gone, but even then I knew he was okay. Two days later, the day before the funeral, I remember waking up and asking my husband, "Do you think they could have made a mistake? Do you think he might just be asleep and not dead?" But I knew that wasn't the case. I was in denial.

Whenever the phone rang, I thought it would be Andy calling me.

The next thing to kick in was guilt. Had I gone straight to the hospital to visit Andy Friday morning instead of going to work first, would things have turned out differently? If I had stayed with him through the surgery instead of going to Kenya, could his blood clot have been avoided? Wow, was I ever thinking an awful lot of myself! I could have changed the course of what happened? Please! Only God can do that. Did I think that I was somehow going to help God? What was I thinking? What's that old expression, "God is in charge, and I'm not"? I felt guilty about things I didn't do, like making sure the hospital staff was watching for blood clots and giving him blood thinners. I felt guilty about nagging him to have the surgery after he had procrastinated about it for so long. I felt guilty for divorcing him two years earlier and breaking his heart, thinking that I had caused the blood clot to throw to his heart. When his surgery was postponed in July due to an irregular heartbeat, I remember crying because I thought it proved that I had actually somehow physically broken Andy's heart. It's funny how after someone dies we tend to forget their annoying traits and remember only their endearing ones. I thought about a Bible passage in Ruth 1:17: "Where you die I will die, and there I will be buried. May the Lord deal with me, be it ever so severely, if anything but death separates you and me."

That first week back at work after the funeral, I had several anxiety or panic attacks. I wasn't thinking about my own death or worrying about dying, but I was worrying about anything and everything else. Loss of a loved one can trigger worries and fears. Things that were happening at work suddenly seemed out of proportion, to the point where I left my job six weeks after Andy died. Whereas ordinarily I could handle anything that came up, I found myself unable to confront issues and address people and problems. I felt insecure. Grief also made its presence known to me through physical symptoms. I fought insomnia, nausea, and fatigue while I was grieving, all of which served to lower my immune system and physically make me sick rather than just making me *feel* sick. I remember telling my husband that I thought I was having a heart attack or that my heart was literally broken. Proverbs tells us that we can find a comparison between a cheerful heart and a sad heart. Have you ever looked at someone's face, especially in their eyes, and just knew that they were heartbroken? I think my heart's condition was written on my face. All I could do was give the situation to the Lord and ask him to give me comfort and strength and take away the sorrow and grief from my heart. There was a hole in my heart that could only be filled by God. Psalm 62:5 tells me, "Find rest, O my soul, in God alone; my hope comes from him."

Although I never went through the anger and bargaining stages, I certainly spent time in the depression stage. As a matter of fact, I have always disliked the word *depressed.* It seemed like such an overused word, like *stressed.* I didn't want to be labeled as depressed. But there wasn't any getting around it. I was there. I was having trouble sleeping, so I was tired all the time. I didn't want to leave the house; I just wanted to crawl under the covers and sleep. I wanted to get lots and lots of sleep. When you're asleep, you can't be depressed. My husband was great; he told me it was okay to cry and be sad. Some people around me were already trying to tell me to "get over it" just a month after my loss. Even though it was embarrassing, I allowed myself to cry when I needed to, even in public. I thought I had to put on a brave face and not be mad or sad. Then I remembered the scripture "Jesus wept" in John 11:35. If it was okay for Jesus to cry when he was sad, wasn't it okay for me to cry? After all, Jesus set the examples for us on how to live. Although I didn't want to admit that I needed help and felt that everything would be okay on its own, I finally did make an appointment and had several sessions with a grief counselor. Talking about my feelings was freeing. Even though I told my husband and friends how I felt, it was different talking to a specialist about my sadness. Scrapbooking all the loose photos of Andy made me feel good. It was healing to creatively arrange the pictures and let the memories behind them wash over me. I also discovered the Internet social-networking site Facebook at that time. I uploaded the photos of Andy and created a photo album on my Facebook profile page and invited friends to browse it. It was my tribute to Andy. Another thing that helped me heal was donating money in Andy's name to his favorite charities and causes.

In church, we learn to be transparent. We have accountability groups to keep us in the light and out of the dark. Whatever we try to hide takes control over our lives. I was determined not to hide my grief and let Satan grab a foothold on my life. Satan wants us to feel alone and isolated because seclusion deepens pain. I made it a point to attend functions and continue to go to church, talk with friends, and seek fellowship with other Christians.

In the movie *The Bucket List*, with Jack Nicholson and Morgan Freeman, the bucket list refers to a list of things each of the two characters wants to see, do, or accomplish before he dies. In one scene, they're visiting the pyramids in Egypt, and Morgan Freeman's character says, 'You know, the ancient Egyptians had a beautiful belief about death. When their souls got to the entrance to heaven, the guards asked two questions. Their answers determined whether they were able to enter or not. "Have you found joy in your life?" "Has your life brought joy to others?"'

Andy had definitely found joy in his life. His joy was found in Christ Jesus. We went with friends to a Billy Graham Crusade in Louisville, Kentucky, in the summer of 2001. Andy and I were both skeptical of what we considered to be televangelists. The only ones we'd ever seen were the bad ones—you know, the ones who get into trouble. But there was something in what Billy Graham said that day and something about that event that stirred Andy's heart. Later, I took comfort in this quote from Billy Graham: "And because we know Christ is alive, we have hope for the present and hope for life beyond the grave." Every Sunday at church when the people getting baptized would repeat the good confession, Andy would say it with them under his breath: "I believe that Jesus is the Christ, the Son of the living God, my Lord and my Savior."

Later that year, Andy attended a free outdoor concert with me where Christian gospel artist Kirk Franklin performed. I was really into Kirk Franklin, and Andy enjoyed listening to some of his CDs when I played them. At one point during the concert, Kirk Franklin asked the audience to find someone in the crowd who was different from themselves and hug them. The crowd was largely African American, and when people turned around, big, tall, Caucasian Andy was like a huge target and they all flocked around him and tried to hug him. It took him by surprise at first, but he finally gave in and just went with it. I think that was the day that Andy started to learn and believe that we are *all* God's children regardless of race.

When Andy went forward in September 2002 to be baptized, it was an answer to prayer for about half a dozen people. Friends and neighbors had seen the great changes in me since becoming a Christian and were shocked at the tremendous positive changes in Andy. Maybe shocked isn't the most accurate word; after all, they knew that God could do anything with anybody, and they had seen positive changes in my life when I became a Christian. Perhaps it was most surprising to those who had known Andy the longest and weren't Christians themselves. He was definitely different after coming up out of that water. He cussed less, he was more patient, and he was slower to anger. He had never complained when I started dragging him to church, and he never skipped church. He had become a more positive, open person as a result of our church attendance and interaction with other Christians. Everybody knew that Andy was stubborn, so for him to humble himself and go forward to accept Christ was a joyous occasion. I had been baptized two years earlier, and he and I had been regularly attending worship services and Bible studies. Friends and neighbors had been praying for Andy. Andy was forty-four years old at the time, but he was like a big kid. Standing six feet four inches and weighing three hundred plus pounds, Andy's only concern about baptism was whether or not the water in the baptismal was going to spill over the sides when he entered it! He had chosen September 15, his birthday, to be born again into Jesus. He was born on September 15, baptized on September 15, and we said good-bye to him at his funeral on September 15.

Andy loved all things having to do with eagles, and I had bought him several items at the local Christian bookstore with eagles and Scripture on them. Thinking about his impending hip surgery, this scripture should have brought him comfort: "But those who hope in the LORD will renew their strength. They will soar on wings like eagles; they will run and not grow weary, they will walk and not be faint" (Isaiah 40:31). At Andy's funeral, when I introduced Andy's dad to the minister, Bob told him that of all things he was thankful for, he was most thankful that I had loved Andy and had brought him to accept a relationship with Jesus.

Likewise, Andy's life had brought joy to others. There was more laughing than crying at Andy's funeral. He had worked for the same employer for twenty-four years, and they shared stories of funny things Andy had said and nice things that Andy had done. Only in the last couple of years had Andy started to feel comfortable enough in his faith to start having conversations about God and church with his coworkers. He had that childlike quality about him, and when he laughed, he laughed that big-belly laugh that everybody got a kick out of hearing. Andy had volunteered as a firefighter for twenty-seven years, and even though he had been retired from volunteering for seven years, many of the firefighters he had served alongside came to his funeral to share how Andy had impacted their lives.

Missing Andy

The nurse in ICU shared the story with us after Andy's passing that as they were wheeling him into the ICU, the nurse struck her head on the IV pole and Andy, instead of worrying about what was going on with him, asked the nurse if she was okay and if there was anything he could do for her. Likewise, when Andy was in his hospital room a few hours before surgery and his roommate was having breathing difficulties, Andy reached out to help the man next to him, whose name he didn't even know. Andy served on the medical team at our church, responding to any incident that occurred during a church service or large event. He had handled everything from church members with shortness of breath and sprained ankles to a little boy who had fallen and whose bone broke through his skin. Andy was a born hero, meant to help and rescue others. I think that's why he spent so many years volunteering as a public servant. Andy definitely brought joy into the lives of others.

THE BIBLE

Unfortunately, I don't read my Bible every day. But when Andy died, I found myself turning to it for comfort and healing. After all the word *Bible* can be an acronym for Basic Instructions Before Leaving Earth. I can't think of any situation that the Bible doesn't tell you how to handle. Just look at Isaiah 61:2–3: "To proclaim the year of the Lord's favor and the day of vengeance of our God, to comfort all who mourn and provide for those who grieve in Zion—to bestow on them a crown of beauty instead of ashes, the oil of gladness instead of mourning, and a garment of praise instead of a spirit of despair. They will be called oaks of righteousness, a planting of the Lord for the display of his splendor." This tells me that I will be comforted in my mourning. As does Jeremiah 31:13, which states, "Then maidens will dance and be glad, young men and old as well. I will turn their mourning into gladness; I will give them comfort and joy instead of sorrow." The book of Psalms has a treasure trove of comforting passages.

Charles Swindoll said, "Trusting God doesn't change our circumstances. Perfect trust in him changes us." Trusting God wasn't going to bring Andy back, but trusting God was going to heal me.

I am grateful to have a relationship with Christ. I didn't become a Christian until my midthirties and sometimes find myself thinking, *Oh, how I wish I had known about Jesus sooner and started living my life for him many years ago.* But you know what? It happens when it's supposed to happen. Dietrich Bonhoeffer said, "Gratitude changes the pangs of memory into a tranquil joy." That is exactly what has happened in my life. The memories of painful past events in my life are erased and replaced by a tranquil joy. The pangs of loss and missing Andy aren't gone, but they're much lighter than they would be if I didn't have a relationship with Jesus and know that Andy was in heaven. I have made that journey from grief to joy.

COMFORTING PSALMS

"I lift up my eyes to the hills—where does my help come from? My help comes from the Lord, the maker of Heaven and earth" (Psalms 121:1–2).

"Blessed is he whose help is the God of Jacob, whose hope is in the Lord his God" (Psalm 146:5).

"You, O Lord, keep my lamp burning; my God turns my darkness into light" (Psalm 18:28).

"Be strong and take heart, all you who hope in the Lord" (Psalm 31:24).

"In my anguish I cried to the Lord, and he answered by setting me free. The Lord is with me; I will not be afraid. What can man do to me?" (Psalms 118:5–6).

BIBLIOGRAPHY

Berg, Alec, Schaeffer, Jeff (Writers) and Ackerman, Andy (Director) (1997). Seinfeld television episode, The Summer of George.

Bonhoeffer, Dietrich (http://www.famousquotesandauthors. com/authors/ dietrich_bonhoeffer_quotes.html retrieved 07/05/2009)

Charles, Oswald, (http://www.brainyquote.com/quotes/quotes/ o/oswaldcham120296.html retrieved 07/05/2009)

Graham, Billy (http://www.gaia.com/quotes/Billy_Graham retrieved 07/05/2009)

Idleman, Kyle, Sermon: Leaving Boldly, Southeast Christian Church, Louisville, KY 09/14/2008

Kubler-Ross, Elisabeth, M.D., On Death and Dying, 1997, Scribner.

Launder, Dale (Writer) and Lynn, Jonathan (Director), (1992), movie My Cousin Vinny.

Moore, Beth (http://blogs.myspace.com/index.cfm?fuseaction =blog.view&friendId=126599950&blogId=354355845 retrieved 07/05/2009)

St. Augustine (http://www.famous-quotes.com/author.php?page=2&total=45&aid=338 retrieved 07/05/2009)

Swindoll, Charles (http://www.brainyquote.com/quotes/authors/c/charles_r_swindoll. html retrieved 07/05/2009)

Tucker, Angie, personal conversation, 2009.

Zackham, Justin (Writer) and Reiner, Rob (Director), movie The Bucket List, 2008.